MUSLIM
Prayer and Worship

Muhammad Ibrahim and Anita Ganeri

SEA-TO-SEA
Mankato Collingwood London

This edition first published in 2008 by
Sea-to-Sea Publications
1980 Lookout Drive
North Mankato
Minnesota 56003

Printed in China

Library of Congress Cataloging in Publication Data:

Ibrahim, Muhammad.
   Muslim prayer and worship / by Muhammad Ibrahim and Anita Ganeri.
      p.cm. -- (Prayer and worship)
   Includes index.
   ISBN 978-1-59771-090-9
   1. Salat--Juvenile literature. 2. Prayer--Islam--Juvenile literature. I. Ganeri, Anita,
1961- II. Title.

BP184.3.I37 2007
297.3'82--dc22
                                                              2006051282

9 8 7 6 5 4 3 2

Published by arrangement with the Watts Publishing Group Ltd, London.

Editor: Rachel Cooke
Design: Joelle Wheelwright

Acknowledgments: Ilyas Dean/Image Works/Topfoto: front cover c, 9. Bernd
Ducke/Superbild/A1 pix: 28. Paul Gapper/World Religions Photo Library: 27. Gaudard/A1
pix: 17. Ali Haider/epa/Corbis: 25. Zainal Ad Halim/Reuters/Corbis: 24. Muhammad
Ibrahim: 6, 8, 10. Gideon Mendel/ Corbis: 16. Kazuyoshi Nomachi/Corbis: 14. Bernd
Obermann/Corbis: 13. Christine Osborne/World Religions Photo Library: 11, 19, 20, 22, 23,
26, 29. Helene Rogers/ArkReligion: front cover b, 4, 5. 15. Claire Stout/World Religions
Photo Library: 12. World Religions Photo Library: 7, 18.

Contents

The prayers in this book were chosen by Muhammad Ibrahim, Head of Religious Studies at Southgate School, London. Muhammad is a practicing Muslim and has been involved in religious education for many years. He is also a member of the Religious Education Council for England and Wales. The formal prayers in this book have been taken directly from the Koran and the Sunnah. Other informal prayers have been adapted from these two sources.

About Islam

Muslims follow the religion of Islam. The word "Islam" means "submission" or "obedience" in the Arabic language. Muslims submit to (obey) the will of God, whom they call Allah, and follow Allah's guidance in all aspects of their lives.

The one true God

Muslims believe that Allah is the one true God who created the world and everything in it. They believe that Islam was the first religion because Allah gave it to Adam, the first man. Adam was the first of many prophets (messengers) chosen by Allah to teach people about Islam. Islam was "completed" by the last and greatest prophet, the Prophet Muhammad (SAWS) who lived in Saudi Arabia about 1,400 years ago. Allah gave the Koran (see page 12) to Muhammad so Islam could never be changed again.

Showing respect

When mentioning the name of the Prophet Muhammad (SAWS), Muslims should always say immediately afterward "*Sallallahu alaihi wasallam*" meaning "Peace and blessings of Allah be upon him." They do this as a sign of respect. In written texts, the phrase is abbreviated to SAWS.

A Muslim girl prays to Allah for guidance.

Muslims around the world

There are about 1.3 billion Muslims in the world, about a quarter of the world's population. They live in many different countries. Indonesia has the largest number of Muslims in the world, followed by India, Pakistan, and Bangladesh.

↑ *The Shahadah is often written in Arabic over the entrance to a mosque, as here. Arabic reads from right to left.*

The Shahadah

La ilaha illallahu Muhammadur rasulullah

There is no god except Allah; Muhammad is Allah's messenger.

About this prayer

This prayer is called the Shahadah. It states what a Muslim believes. Firstly, it states that there is only one God and no other. At a simple level, in everyday life, this means not treating people, like celebrities or sports stars, or objects like money, as gods. Secondly, it states that Muhammad (SAWS) is a Prophet of Allah. Someone can become a Muslim by saying and believing in the Shahadah. But they must take their commitment seriously, believe in the Shahadah honestly and try to put it into practice throughout their lives.

Muslim Prayer and Worship

In Arabic, the word for worship is "Ibadah," which means being in the service of Allah. Muslims believe Allah calls everyone to worship Him. Ibadah is for Allah alone, which is why Muslims should only pray to Allah.

Saying prayers

Prayer is a very important part of a Muslim's daily life. Every good Muslim must perform their prayers five times a day (see right). These set prayers are called "Salah" (see page 8). It was the angel Jibril who taught Muhammad (SAWS) how to pray. Muslims can also say personal prayers at any time. These are called "Du'a" and are a way of calling on Allah. The Prophet Muhammad would say Du'a silently or aloud with others, so Muslims do either today. They pray to Allah for help and guidance.

This special clock helps Muslims work out the times for prayer.

So glory be to Allah,
When you reach the
evening
And when you rise in
the morning:
Yes, to Him be praise,
In the heavens and
on earth;
And in the late
afternoon
And when the day
begins to decline.

About this prayer

These two verses come from the Koran (30:17-18). They describe the times at which a Muslim should pray their Salah. Muslims pray because Allah has told them to and because they gain great benefit from it. They pray as if they are standing in the presence of Allah.

The five set prayer times are:

1) Fajr: Early in the morning at dawn.
2) Zuhr: At midday when the sun has just passed its highest point.
3) Asr: In midafternoon when your shadow is the same length as your body.
4) Magrib: Just after sunset.
5) Isha: After sunset and before midnight.

The Hadith

Muslims sometimes like to say the same prayers as Muhammad (SAWS). These can be found in books, called the Hadith, which contain the sayings of Muhammad (SAWS) (see page 15).

A Muslim child learns to pray. Muslim children start to pray at about seven years old. They should be praying regularly by the time they are 10.

Set Prayers

The set prayers Muslims say five times a day are called "Salah." The word "Salah" comes from the Arabic for "to communicate." By saying their prayers, Muslims believe they are communicating directly with Allah.

For Wudu, Muslims wash their face, hands, and feet, and also wipe their heads.

Five Pillars of Islam

Salah is the second of the Five Pillars of Islam. These are five duties that help Muslims put their beliefs into practice. Carrying out the Five Pillars shows Muslims are putting their faith above everything else in their lives. The Five Pillars are:

1 The Shahadah: declaration of faith (see page 5)
2 Salah: five daily prayers
3 Zakah: money paid to help others
4 Sawm: fasting in the month of Ramadan (see page 26)
5 Hajj: pilgrimage to Makkah (see page 24).

Preparing for prayer

Before Salah, Muslims must prepare themselves for prayer. They must put aside all other thoughts and concentrate on Allah. If they do not, their prayers will not be worthwhile. They must also wear clean clothes and wash themselves in a special way. This washing is called "Wudu" and it is part of the act of worship. Wudu helps make the worshipper clean in both body and mind.

8

Words and movements

As Muslims say the words of the prayers, they perform a series of set movements. Each set of movements is called a rak'ah. There is a set number of rak'ahs for each time of prayer. These words and movements were taught by the Prophet Muhammad (SAWS) to the first Muslims and have not changed since that time. They are copied by all Muslims all over the world. The panel below shows a selection of movements and words made and said when Muslims pray their Salah.

1 **Qiyam.** Muslims stand upright with both hands raised up to their ears. They recite "Allahu Akbar," which means "God is the Greatest." They place their left hands on their chests with their right hands on top. Then they recite certain verses from the Koran.

2 **Ruku**. Muslims bow at the waist and place their hands on their knees. They say: "Sami' allahu liman hamidah," meaning "Our Lord, praise be to You."

3 **Sujud**. This is when Muslims kneel with their hands and faces on the ground. Seven parts of the body should touch the ground (two sets of toes, two knees, two hands, and the face). In this position, the Muslim says: "Subhana rabbiyal a'la," which means "Glory to my Lord, the Highest."

4 At the end of Salah, Muslims rise to a kneeling position with their hands on their knees. They turn their heads first to the right, then to the left, and offer the person on either side this greeting: "Assalamu alaikum wa rahmatullah," which means "Peace and the Mercy of Allah be upon you."

A group of Muslims pray together. They are at different stages of their Salah.

9

Worship in the Mosque

A Muslim place for prayer is called a mosque. The Arabic word for mosque is "masjid." Mosques are usually thought of as buildings where Muslims can come together to pray. But anywhere that a Muslim chooses for prayer is believed to become a mosque for that particular time.

Mosques need not take on any specific shape or form. Some are built for the purpose, like this one in Palmer's Green, London, England, which is almost complete. Others are converted from other buildings.

Call to prayer

Muslim daily prayers start with the call to prayer, which is given from the minaret of the mosque. This is called the "Adhan" (see page 23). The call to prayer is given by a person called a "Mu'adhin." Traditionally, a Mu'adhin would call from a minaret tower, but today, in some countries, he can be heard through a loudspeaker. Muslim women are not expected to go to the mosque, although they can if they wish to. They usually say their prayers at home. Muslim men should attend the mosque at least once a week for midday prayers on Fridays.

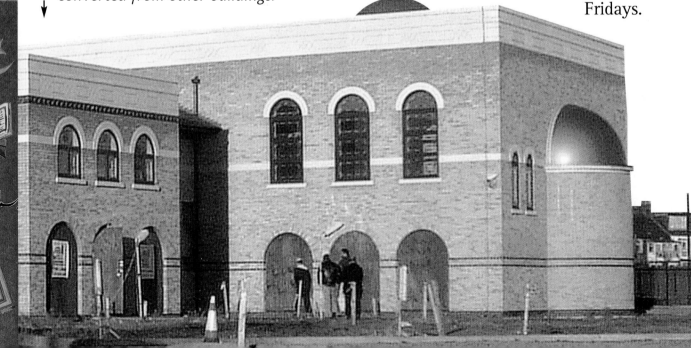

Friday prayers

Fridays are special days to Muslims. They believe that Allah created Adam, the first man, on a Friday. This makes Fridays a time for Muslims to remember the precious gift of life that Allah has given. Midday prayers on Fridays are called "Jumu'ah" which means "gathering." If possible, all Muslim men try to attend the mosque. They believe that praying with others in the mosque will bring greater blessings and help to build up a stronger community spirit.

When Muslims pray, they must turn to face the Ka'bah in Makkah in Saudi Arabia. This direction is called "qiblah." In many mosques, the qiblah wall is marked by a qiblah arch.

O you who believe,
When you hear the call
to prayer on Friday.
Go quickly to remember Allah.
Leave your business
(or what you are doing)
That is best for you, if you but knew.

And when the Prayer is finished,
You can go back through the land,
Seek the goodness of Allah,
And remember Allah often so that
you may do well.

About this prayer

These verses come from the Koran (62:9-10). They tell Muslims that when they hear the call to prayer on Friday, they must go to the mosque and remember Allah. Afterward, they should remember Allah when they go back to their daily tasks. On a Friday, the midday prayer called "Zuhr" is replaced with the Jumu'ah prayer, which will include a talk by the Imam. He is a senior person who leads the prayers in the mosque. The talk helps to remind people of their duties as good Muslims.

Prayers from the Koran

Many of the prayers used in Muslim worship come from the Koran. This is the sacred book of the Muslims. They believe that the Koran is the direct word of Allah and treat it with great respect. They believe the Koran was revealed in Arabic as a guide to help Muslims live their lives properly.

Reading aloud

Muslims should not simply read the Koran but should try to put its teachings into practice. In Arabic, the word "Koran" means "to read out loud." That is why, as part of Muslim prayer, verses from the Koran are often recited out loud. Even if listeners do not understand every word, they may be inspired by hearing them.

Two Muslim boys in Kenya read from the Koran. The script is Arabic.

12

The Koran

Muslims believe Allah gave the verses of the Koran to the Prophet Muhammad (SAWS) over many years. Muhammad could not read or write but memorized the words. He also recited them to his companions who learned them by heart. After Muhammad's death, they collected all the verses together and wrote them down in one book. The verses were not changed in any way and have not been changed since.

↑ *A Qari recites from the Koran at a mosque. A Qari is a hafiz (someone who has learned the Koran by heart).*

In the name of Allah, the Kindest and Most Merciful. Praise is for Allah, Master of the Universe, The Kindest and Most Merciful One, King of the Day of Judgment. You are the One we worship; You are the One we ask for help. Show us the straight path; The path of those whom You are pleased with, Not the path of those who deserve Your anger, Nor those who become lost.

About this prayer

The Koran is divided into 114 surahs (chapters), made up of 6,616 ayats (verses). These are the first verses of the Koran (1: 1-7). They are called "Al-Fatihah" ("The Opening") and are a prayer to Allah for guidance. The rest of the Koran is the answer to this prayer. Muslims recite these verses during each rak'ah of their Salah so they say them many times a day. The verses express the Muslim belief that Allah is the only one they should worship. They also ask Allah for help and guidance in living their life in a way that pleases Him.

Prayer of Light

Muslims believe that the Koran is the word of Allah. But it can only make sense if we can understand it. People have different experiences in different times and places. To understand the Koran, it is important to try to understand what it was like for people living at the time of the Prophet Muhammad (SAWS).

The city of Makkah where Muhammad was born.

The life of the Prophet

The Prophet Muhammad (SAWS) lived from 570-632 C.E. in the country we now call Saudi Arabia. Muslims try hard to follow the example of what he said and how he lived. This example is known as the "Sunnah" and it is written down in the Hadith (see next page). It is a rich and valuable source of prayers and inspiration for Muslims. For example, if Muslims have a problem, they turn to the Sunnah or the Koran to see what Muhammad might have done in a similar situation. This might mean trying to find a rule to deal with a modern activity, such as smoking. Muslims are not allowed to smoke because smoking can kill you and the Sunnah shows that it is wrong to kill yourself.

O Allah, place light in my heart, and on my tongue light, and in my ears light and in my sight light, and above me light, and below me light, and to my right light and behind me light. Place in my soul light. Magnify for me light, and amplify for me light. Make for me light and make me a light. O Allah, grant me light, and place light in my nerves, and in my body light and in my blood light and in my hair light and in my skin light. O Allah, make for me a light in my grave... and a light in my bones. Increase me in light, increase in me light, increase in me light. Grant me light upon light.

About this prayer

The words of this prayer are part of the Sunnah. They come from books called the Hadith, which are collections of the Prophet Muhammad (SAWS)'s sayings and accounts of his actions. They were put together after Muhammad's death to report the Sunnah and record what reliable people remembered of Muhammad's life. This prayer talks about light or truth, which is an important symbol of hope and inspiration. Muslims may either think or recite it when they pray their Du'a (private prayers to Allah).

This is a shortened volume of a collection of Hadith made by Sahih Al-Bukhari.

- - - - ->

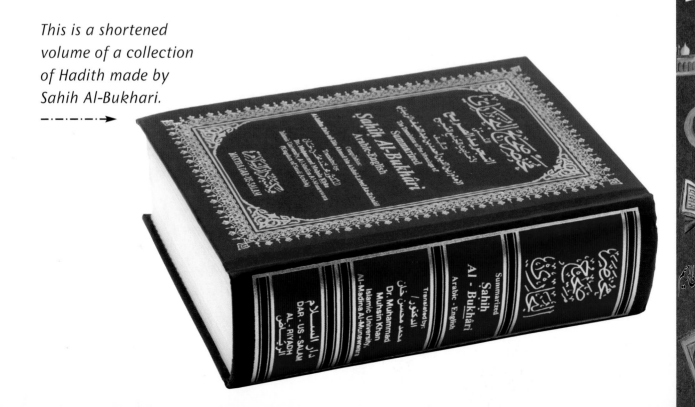

Prayer for Forgiveness

Everyone makes mistakes and does things that they regret. But Muslims believe that Allah will forgive anyone who is genuinely sorry for what they have done and who promises to try to do better in future. Forgiveness is a very important quality in Islam.

Thinking of others

Islam teaches that when we do good things, it not only helps ourselves but also others. Similarly doing bad things can hurt many people. We must make the effort to say sorry and encourage others to make the effort to forgive us.

A group of children play together. Even when you play, you need to think of others.

The names of Allah

In Arabic, one of the names for Allah is "Al Ghaffar," which means "the Great Forgiver." Muslims believe that Allah has many names. Each of them tells us about one of Allah's qualities. For example, Allah may be called "Ar Rahman," which means "the Most Compassionate," or "Al Karim," which means "the Generous One." Trying to develop these qualities, and to be more compassionate or generous, will help us live our lives in a better way and make the world a better place.

A Muslim girl says a private prayer (Du'a). She may include the prayer below.

"To make things easy"

Do not punish us if we do things that are wrong because of forgetfulness or because we do not know that they are wrong. Please do not make things as difficult for us as you have done to those before us. Help us to cope with those things we find too difficult. Forgive us when we do those things that are wrong. We know you are looking after us. Help us to help those who do not understand this.

About this prayer

This prayer is adapted from the Koran (2:286). It may be said at anytime when Muslims pray their Du'a. The Koranic verse itself may be recited as part of Salah after the Al-Fatihah. Often this verse is written on cards for Muslims to read whenever they feel worried, when things have gone wrong or someone has died. It helps to give them comfort so that they can cope. It asks Allah to help us in difficult times and to forgive us if we do something wrong.

17

Rules to Live By

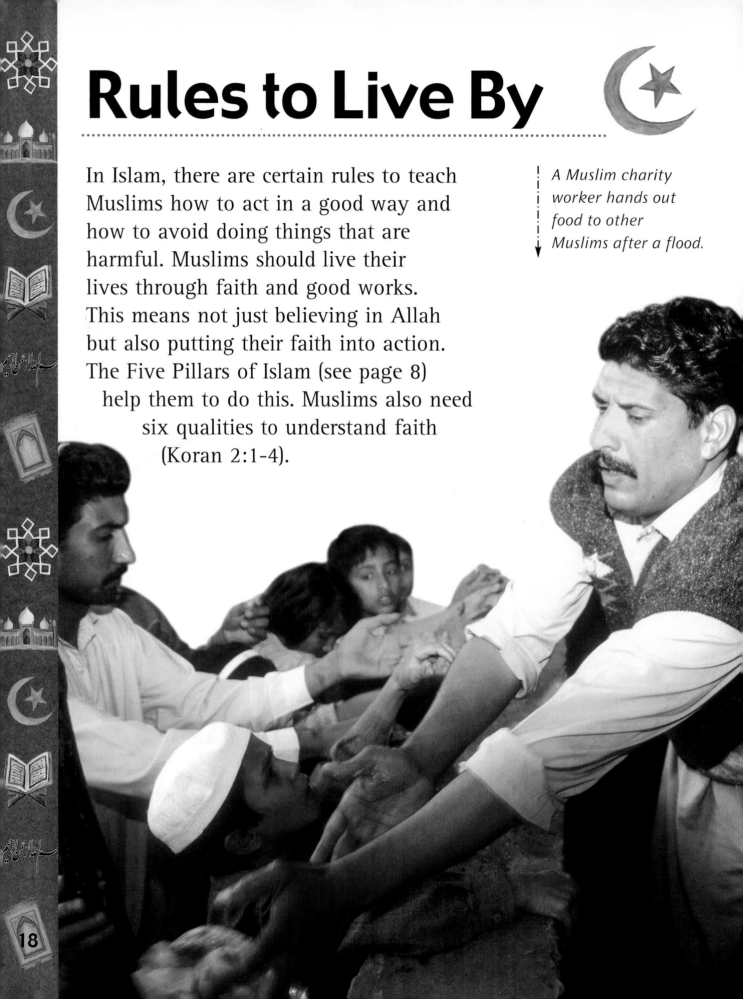

In Islam, there are certain rules to teach Muslims how to act in a good way and how to avoid doing things that are harmful. Muslims should live their lives through faith and good works. This means not just believing in Allah but also putting their faith into action. The Five Pillars of Islam (see page 8) help them to do this. Muslims also need six qualities to understand faith (Koran 2:1-4).

A Muslim charity worker hands out food to other Muslims after a flood.

Six Qualities for Faith

1 **Piety**—knowing how to live as a good, kind person.

2 **Ghayb**—believing in things beyond our understanding, such as Allah, paradise, and angels.

3 **Salah**—being able to pray five times a day, every day.

4 **Giving freely**—believing that your life is not your own, to do as you please, but seeing it as a loan from Allah and using it responsibly to please Allah and help others.

5 **Revelations**—Allah has given guidance to humans to help them know what is right and wrong. Books such as the Koran are examples of such guidance.

6 **Akhirah**—believing in a life after death.

*O Allah, I pray that I can listen to
and be obedient to your guidance,
So that through my bad or
thoughtless behavior I may not
encourage others to do the same.
Or that I too may not be
misguided by them,
Or that I cause others to avoid
doing good things,
Or they cause me to do harm,
Or that I abuse other people,
Or that they abuse me,
Or that I behave foolishly
Or indeed meet the foolishness of
their behavior.
Help me to encourage others
to do good things,
So that they can encourage me
to do good things,*

*So that I can be kind to others,
So that they will be kind to me,
So that I can behave
with thought and care,
So that they can meet my
behavior with thought and care,
Help me to encourage others not
to do silly things.*

About this prayer

Muslims use the teachings of the Koran and the Sunnah as guides for living their lives. This prayer is taken from the Hadith. It could be said as a private prayer by someone leaving home to go to school or work and asking for Allah's guidance in the day ahead. It reminds Muslims to be kind and helpful to others, and to set a good example by their own good deeds.

19

Family Prayers

Family life is an important part of Islam. It is vital to look after our families because then society will look after itself. A large part of this belief is showing love and respect to our parents and teachers because they will be the ones teaching us to become caring, kind, and wise.

The Ummah

Muslims are asked to consider their actions carefully. They are not just responsible for their own actions but for the effect of their actions on the whole community. In Islam, the community is known as the "Ummah," which means the worldwide family of Muslims.

A Muslim family gathers for a meal.

Praying together

Since Salah has set prayers, it means that millions of Muslims across the world say the same prayers every day. This helps Muslims feel part of a much wider family as well as their own.

In Islam an elderly man is given the title "Sheik" to mean someone who is wise and learned.

"To respect my parents and my teachers"

Help me to learn not to be so selfish and to think carefully about why my parents and my teachers want me to do well.
Help me to be kind to my parents and to those who care for me.
Help me to want to care for my parents when they get old.
Encourage me not to say anything that will make them angry.
Encourage me not to say bad things to them, nor to shout at them.
Encourage me to speak to them softly with kind words of honor and respect.

Encourage me to be humble and kind when they are angry with me, as I know they love me and want me to do well.

About this prayer

This prayer is adapted from a selection of verses from the Koran and the Hadith. It may be said as a private prayer. Muslim children are encouraged to think carefully about those who are older than them. Parents and teachers should speak with respect and set a good example to those who are in their care. In turn, children should show love and respect to their elders. They should not answer back or disobey people who are trying to help them. They should honor their parents and care for them in old age.

Prayers for the Birth of a Baby

For Muslims, a baby is a gift from Allah and parents have a special responsibility to look after their children. From an early age, parents teach their children to be good Muslims, to learn about their faith, and to work hard and care for others.

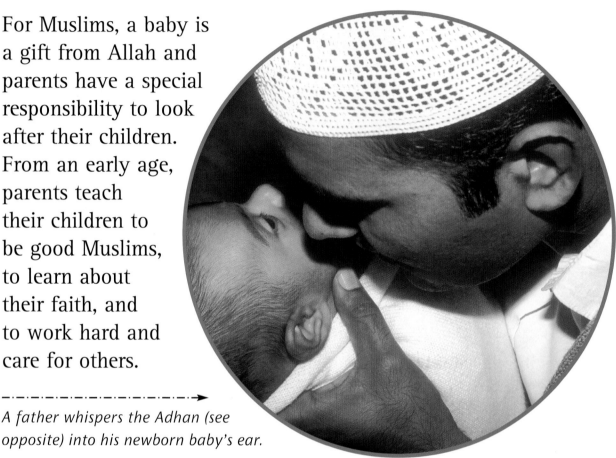

A father whispers the Adhan (see opposite) into his newborn baby's ear.

Choosing a name

When a baby is born, a ceremony called "Aqiqah" is held to give the child its name. Muslims believe it is important to give children a name with a good meaning. Many Muslim boys are named after the Prophet Muhammad (SAWS). Others are given one of the names of Allah, such as Hafiz (Protector) or Karim (Generous).

"Abdul," meaning servant, is added in front of these names because it is wrong to call someone "Allah." So the name "Abdul Hafiz" means "Servant of the Protector." Many Muslim girls are named after famous early Muslim women who were followers of Muhammad or members of his family.

Allah is the Greatest, Allah is the Greatest,
Allah is the Greatest, Allah is the Greatest,
I bear witness that there
is no god but Allah,
I bear witness that there
is no god but Allah,
I bear witness that Muhammad
is Allah's messenger,
I bear witness that Muhammad
is Allah's messenger,
Rush to prayer, Rush to prayer,
Rush to success, Rush to success,
Allah is the Greatest,
Allah is the Greatest.

About this prayer

This prayer is called the Adhan (the call to prayer). It is called out from the mosque in Arabic before every Salah. It is also said when a Muslim baby is born. The father whispers the Adhan into the baby's right ear so that the first word the baby is likely to hear will be "Allah." Just as the Adhan calls Muslims to prayer, it also calls the baby to a life of prayer and devotion to Allah.

↑ *A Mu'adhin standing in a minaret tower calls people to prayer with the Adhan.*

23

Hajj Prayers

Once a year, more than two million Muslims gather in and around the city of Makkah in Saudi Arabia to celebrate the pilgrimage called Hajj. Hajj is one of the Five Pillars of Islam and all Muslims try to make Hajj at least once in their lifetimes. Muslims believe that the first time they perform Hajj, all of their sins are washed away. Hajj gives Muslims a chance for a fresh start.

*Here I am at Your service, O Allah
You have no partner
Here I am at Your service, O Allah
Verily, all the praise, the grace belong to You,
And the kingdom.
You have no partner.*

About this prayer
This prayer is recited by Muslims many times during Hajj. It is called "Talbiyah," which means "to follow" or "to obey." It is one of the prayers said by the Prophet Muhammad (SAWS) when he was performing Hajj. Muslims start reciting this prayer when they reach the Ka'bah in the center of the great mosque in Makkah. The Ka'bah is the most important building in Islam and Muslims turn to face it when they pray.

Muslims walking and praying around the Ka'bah in Makkah.

The route of Hajj

When pilgrims arrive in Makkah, they walk around the Ka'bah seven times. Then they walk or run between two nearby hills and visit the well of Zamzam. This reminds them of the story of Hajar (the wife of the Prophet Ibrahim) who had to search in the desert for water for her son. Later, the pilgrims gather on the Plain of Arafat where the Prophet Muhammad (SAWS) gave his last sermon. This is the main part of Hajj. Here the pilgrims stand and pray for forgiveness for their sins. After this, at a place called Mina, they throw stones at three pillars which stand for the devil.

Pilgrims dressed in ihram pray on the Plain of Arafat.

Pilgrims' dress

During Hajj, pilgrims wear special clothes called "ihram." All men wear two plain white sheets of cloth. One is worn around the waist; the other around the shoulders. There is no set dress for women. They wear their ordinary, modest clothes. Wearing similar clothes shows that everyone is equal in Allah's eyes. This is important for Muslims. They believe that, on the Day of Judgment, Allah will judge everyone on their good or bad deeds, not on whether they are rich or poor. Allah teaches that everyone is equal apart from those who do a greater number of good deeds.

Prayers for Id

The two main festivals in Islam are Id-ul-Fitr and Id-ul-Adha. The Prophet Muhammad (SAWS) spoke of Id-ul-Adha as being the more important of the two. The word "Id" means "feast" or "celebration." These two festivals are especially happy times when Muslims celebrate their faith and give thanks to Allah.

A Muslim makes an Id gift of money called "Zakat-ul-Fitr."

Id-ul-Adha

The festival of Id-ul-Adha takes place at the end of the Hajj pilgrimage. Its name means "festival of the sacrifice." At this time, Muslims remember the story of how the Prophet Ibrahim was ready to kill his son, Isma'il, to show his willingness to obey Allah. Allah told Ibrahim that he had proved his love and gave him a ram to sacrifice instead. Today, Muslims still sacrifice a sheep or goat. Some of the meat is shared out among family and friends. Some is given to the poor so they too can enjoy an Id feast.

Id-ul-Fitr

Id-ul-Fitr marks the end of Ramadan, the month of fasting. During this time, Muslims do not eat or drink during the hours of daylight. They will only eat after sunset and before it starts to get light in the morning. Id-ul-Fitr is a time when Muslims work hard to make their community better and stronger. To help bring this about, they make a special gift of money to Muslims who are poor and needy.

When we are down, or upset, we sometimes do things because we are angry.

When we are up, or happy, we sometimes do things because we want to share our happiness.

We often do things to tell others how we feel.

A nasty stare or frown will tell others we are unhappy.

A gentle kiss or a smiling face will show we are happy.

A kiss or a smile is one of the greatest gifts we can give in charity.

All of this will amount to nothing unless we strive to have a good heart.

We should strive to please others because we want to please them.

We should strive to please God because we want to please Him.

We should try to be genuine, honest and sincere in all that we do.

About this prayer

On Id morning, Muslims go to the mosque for Id prayers. They pray two rak'ahs, then listen to a talk given by the Imam. Afterward, they visit relatives, friends, and neighbors to exchange gifts and wish them a happy Id. Id is a time of happiness for everyone to share.

The prayer above is one Muslims might say in private after Salah at Id. Its message is that our good deeds mean nothing unless we mean them sincerely.

↑ *Muslims celebrate Id by exchanging gifts with their family and friends.*

Final Prayers

The first word a Muslim baby should hear is "Allah" (see pages 22–23). When a Muslim is dying, he or she should try to say the Shahadah (see page 5) so that the last word he or she says is also "Allah." When a Muslim hears of the death of someone they should say: "*To Allah we belong, and to Him we return.*" In this way, Allah should be at the heart of a Muslim's life from its beginning to its end.

The Islamic gardens of the Alhambra Palace in Spain. Muslims believe paradise (see next page) to be like a beautiful garden.

Day of Judgment

Muslims believe that on the Day of Judgment, they can hope to be reunited with their loved ones. This gives great comfort to a dying person and to their loved ones. On the Day of Judgment, Allah will judge everyone according to how they have lived. Good people will be rewarded with paradise. Wicked people will be punished in hell. Muslims must remember that paradise is not given automatically. It has to be worked for. They also know that Allah is a good and merciful judge, ready to forgive people if they are truly sorry for their wrongdoings.

↑ *A Muslim recites prayers at a grave.*

The Funeral Prayers
Salah is prayed without full prostrations.
The following Du'a may be said:
O Allah forgive us, both those who are alive and those who have died;
Those who are near to us and those who are far away;
Keep those of us who are here to always remain true to Your will;
Keep those who are dying firm and strong in their faith.

As the body is lowered into the ground, the following is said:
In the name of Allah, we commit you to this earth, according to the Way of the Prophet of Allah.

About this prayer
These are a selection of the prayers recited at a Muslim's funeral. Muslims have to be buried, not cremated. This is because Muslims believe that their bodies will lie in the grave until the Day of Judgment. They are buried facing toward the city of Makkah. The final prayers are called "Salat ul Janaza," which means "funeral prayers." These are the same words as the daily Salah but Muslims do not prostrate themselves on the ground. Being aware of death helps Muslims to focus on what life is for, that is to gain Allah's blessing.

Glossary

Adhan The words of the call to prayer made from the mosque before each prayer time. They are also whispered into a newborn baby's ear.

Al-Fatihah The first, or opening, chapter of the Koran.

Allah The Islamic name for God in the Arabic language.

Arabic The religious language of Islam. The Koran is written in Arabic and Muslims pray in Arabic.

Du'a Personal prayers said by Muslims. The word "Du'a" means "call" or "summon" and these prayers are a way of calling on Allah.

Hadith The sayings and actions of the Prophet Muhammad (SAWS). These were reported by people who knew him and written down later.

Hafiz The title given to someone who has learned the Koran off by heart.

Hajj The annual pilgrimage to Makkah, one of the Five Pillars of Islam.

Ibadah The Arabic word for all acts of worship. It means any actions performed in the service of Allah, including prayers.

Id The Arabic for festival or holiday.

Imam A person who leads prayers in the mosque and gives a talk at Friday midday prayers.

Islam The religion given by Allah for humans to follow, in order to gain peace. Followers of Islam are called Muslims.

Jumu'ah The weekly prayers performed by Muslims in the mosque shortly after midday on a Friday. The word "Jumu'ah" means "to collect" or "unite."

Ka'bah The cube-shaped building in the center of the grand mosque in Makkah. It is the holiest building in Islam. Muslims turn to face it when they say their prayers.

Makkah The city where the Prophet Muhammad (SAWS) was born and where the Ka'bah is found. Muslims visit Makkah to perform the Hajj pilgrimage.

Minaret A tower attached to a mosque from which the Adhan is given.

Mosque A place of Muslim prayer. The Arabic word for mosque is "masjid," which means a place of prostration (bowing down before Allah).

Mu'adhin The person who gives the call to prayer. It is sometimes spelled Muezzin.

Prophets Special people chosen by Allah to act as His messengers and to teach people about His wishes.

Koran The holy book of Islam revealed (given) to the Prophet Muhammad (SAWS) by Allah.

Rak'ah A unit of the set words and movements of Salah prayer.

Ramadan The month of fasting in the Islamic calendar.

Salah The formal prayers Muslims perform five times a day.

SAWS Short for "*Sallallahu alaihi wasallam,*" meaning "Peace and blessings of Allah be upon him." Muslims should always say this immediately after mentioning Muhammad (SAWS) by name.

Shahadah The declaration of faith. It sums up what Muslims believe about Allah and about Muhammad (SAWS).

Sunnah The words, actions, and customs of the Prophet Muhammad (SAWS). These are written down in the Hadith. Muslims use them as a guide for their lives and worship.

Further information

Books to read

Sacred Texts: The Koran
Anita Ganeri, Evans Brothers 2003

Muslim Festivals Through the Year
Anita Ganeri, Franklin Watts 2003

Religion in Focus: Islam
Geoff Teece, Franklin Watts 2003

Keystones: Muslim Mosque
Umar Hegedus, A & C Black 2000

World Religions: Islam
Richard Tames, Franklin Watts 1999

Websites

www.mcb.org.uk
The website of the Muslim Council of Britain.

www.islamic-foundation.org.uk
The Islamic Foundation's website, including additional resources.

www.iqratrust.org
Website of Iqra Trust, a Muslim educational charity.

www.islamic-relief.org.uk
Website of Islamic Relief, an international aid organization.

Index